Baby Zoo Animals

APR 2011

Jane Katirgis

Bailey Books
an imprint of
Enslow Publishers, Inc.
40 Industrial Road
Box 398
Berkeley Heights, NJ 07922
USA
http://www.enslow.com

21.25

Bailey Books, an imprint of Enslow Publishers, Inc.

Library of Congress Cataloging-in-Publication Data

Katirgis, Jane.
 Baby zoo animals / Jane Katirgis.
   p. cm. — (All about baby animals)
 Includes bibliographical references and index.
 Summary: "Introduces simple concepts about zoo animals using short sentences
and repetition of words"—Provided by publisher.
 ISBN 978-0-7660-3796-0
 1. Zoo animals—Infancy—Juvenile literature. I. Title.
 SF408.K38 2011
 636.088'9—dc22
                              2010011896
Paperback ISBN: 978-1-59845-509-0

Printed in the United States of America

052010 Lake Book Manufacturing, Inc., Melrose Park, IL

10 9 8 7 6 5 4 3 2 1

To Our Readers: We have done our best to make sure all Internet Addresses in this book
were active and appropriate when we went to press. However, the author and the publisher
have no control over and assume no liability for the material available on those Internet sites
or on other Web sites they may link to. Any comments or suggestions can be sent by e-mail
to comments@enslow.com or to the address on the back cover.

♻ Enslow Publishers, Inc., is committed to printing our books on recycled paper. The paper
in every book contains 10% to 30% post-consumer waste (PCW). The cover board on the
outside of each book contains 100% PCW. Our goal is to do our part to help young people
and the environment too!

Photo Credits: iStockphoto.com: © Andrew J Shearer, p. 12, © camillaskye, p. 10, © Jason
Krzyzanowski, p. 14, © moodville, p. 8, © Paul Erickson, pp. 3 (nap), 16, © Peter Malsbury,
pp. 1, 18, 22, © Philip Dyer, pp. 3 (hug), 6; Shutterstock.com, pp. 3 (zoo), 4, 20.

Cover Photo: © Jason Krzyzanowski/ iStockphoto.com

Note to Parents and Teachers
Help pre-readers get a jumpstart on reading. These lively stories introduce simple concepts
with repetition of words and short simple sentences. Photos and illustrations fill the pages
with color and effectively enhance the text. Free Educator Guides are available for this series
at www.enslow.com. Search for the *All About Baby Animals* series name.

Contents

Words to Know

hug   **nap**   **zoo**

What is new at the zoo?

**A baby hugs
at the zoo.**

A baby naps at the zoo.

A baby walks at the zoo.

A baby eats
at the zoo.

**A baby hugs
at the zoo.**

A baby naps at the zoo.

A baby walks at the zoo.

A baby eats at the zoo.

A baby grows up at the zoo.

Read More

Kalman, Bobbie. *Living Things in My Backyard.* New York: Crabtree Publishing Co., 2007.

Kirby, Pamela F. *What Bluebirds Do.* Honesdale, Penn.: Boyds Mills Press, 2009.

Web Sites

National Geographic. *Animals.*
<http://animals.nationalgeographic.com>
Click on "Animal Photos."

National Wildlife Federation. *Wild Animal Baby.*
<http://www.nwf.org/Kids.aspx>
Click on "Wild Animal Baby."

Index

Guided Reading Level: B
Guided Reading Leveling System is based on the guidelines recommended by Fountas and Pinnell.
Word Count: 61